The Other Side of the Clouds

W. Joseph Dupuis

authorHOUSE®

AuthorHouse™
1663 Liberty Drive, Suite 200
Bloomington, IN 47403
www.authorhouse.com
Phone: 1-800-839-8640

First published by AuthorHouse 2/20/2009

ISBN: 978-1-4389-5312-0 (sc)

*Printed in the United States of America
Bloomington, Indiana*

This book is printed on acid-free paper.

Foreword

Imagine a journey to the other side of the clouds. A journey filled with visions of great achievement and bountiful reward. Imagine living a dream where all that you dream is accomplished, and the sweet nectar of success is yours to savor at every enterprise.

Come with me, as we journey through the sorrows of failure and the delectable sweetness of success on our way to the other side of the clouds.

This story is dedicated to my children and grandchildren that they will know me for who I am and what I have achieved. I want this story to serve as testimony to the fact that a person can be whatever one wants to be. Everyone is allowed to dream. Dreams are what drive us to accomplishments. But dreams alone can not achieve anything. To live a dream, one must set goals, attainable goals. It is not enough to wish for or to want for. A dream without goals is only a wish, and wishes do not come true.

My dream was to see the other side of the clouds and I went about it the wrong way. I set up obstacles for myself which I would have to overcome in order to realize my dream.

This is my lesson to you. Failure is not the end. It is the beginning of another opportunity to succeed. Develop a dream. Set realistic goals, and work hard, no matter what sacrifices you will have to make to achieve your goals. The other side of the clouds is not a place, it is an accomplishment.

To my daughters, grandchildren...
...and to Amy.

Chapter One

Clouds

*T*he clover field was soft and lush green, and it felt cool, as I lay on my back looking up at the sky. I could hear a Meadow Lark singing in the distance. The honey bees were buzzing by my head on their search for pollen in the green clover field. The sun was high on that mid-afternoon warm day in May. The sky was clear and bright blue save for a few cumulus clouds that hung directly overhead. I wondered what clouds looked like on the other side. The clouds held a mystery from me. What were they made of, I wondered. From where did they come? Where were they going? What was on the other side?

Sometime the clouds seem so heavy as if someone could stand on them and walk through the sky. Sometime the clouds moved very slowly, ever-changing. The thick clouds moved upward in a seemingly angry way to form images.

They formed an image of an angry old man, or the soft gentle face of a kindly young woman. Then ever so slowly they changed into the image of a beautiful horse or playful dog. They beckoned to me. Wanting me to stay and watch. The clouds were forever changing, providing hours of silent rapture for my eyes as I lay on my back in the clover field near the house where we lived in Louisiana.

The House

I was born Weldon Joseph Dupuis on January 10, 1943, the seventh child of Leroy J. and Alix Dupuis. At the time of my birth, my family lived in a rural community just outside the town of Ville Platte, Louisiana. My father was a farmer, though he had no land, he was hired as a sharecropper by land owners. He and my elder brothers worked the fields for a share of the produce and a place to live. Most of the crop was corn, potatoes, rice and cotton. The only farm implements were horse-drawn plows, shovels, rakes and hoes. The work was laborious with long hours in the fields.

The people engaged in this labor had been working the fields for generations, and it was likely that they would remain at this occupation for generations to come. The lack of industry in the area perpetuated this life of the commoner. I was the fourth son in the family and was destined to work the fields as my brothers did. Only education and a strong desire for a better life could prevent the cycle from continuing.

The town of Ville Platte is small, only 20,000 inhabitants. It has a post office, one small supermarket, two movie theaters, and a court house. Ville Platte is the Parrish Seat for Evangeline Parrish. We had two 5 & 10 cents stores. One had a soda jerk. The main department stores, two of them, G. Ardion's and West Brothers were on Main Street Everything was on Main Street.

Five miles from town was the only industry in the entire Parrish, the Conoco Oil and Carbon Black plants. For industrial jobs, men had to go to the Gulf of Mexico to seek employment on off shore oil drilling rigs.

It was in the spring of 1946 when we moved into the house which sat in the middle of the fields. I was only three years old, but I can remember much of that time. Two large oak trees grew in the front. One, a live oak, which kept its leaves all year, and the other was a very tall white oak. A large pond was near the tall white oak, and another off to the left of the live oak. The smaller pond had an irrigation ditch coming into and out of it. I know it was springtime because the water in the irrigation ditch was not running. A barbed wire fence circled the house and another wooden fence enclosed the barnyard and barn. Fields and pastures were all around the house and crops grew almost year round. Cattle lingered near the pond during the day. When the daytime temperature rose, the cattle slowly walked into the water in order to keep cool. Then, they gathered under the live oak tree to take comfort in the shade. The ground around the trees and pond was bare from the moving about of the herd of cattle. Not a blade of grass. During midday, the heat from the barren ground rose. The humidity and the smell of cow manure were heavy. Then in the early evening, the moist air filled with dust hung on the horizon. The moist air hung above the ground in a heavy mist. The air cooled and the mist over the open fields fell to the grass as dew dampening the ground.

At night the house was dark, save for the kerosene lanterns on the fireplace mantel. On warmer evenings the whole family sat on the huge front porch. Mom and Dad had each a rocking chair, and the rest of the older siblings fought for the remaining rockers.

Our family was considered large. We were four boys and four girls. My brother Swarn, was the oldest, followed by Waverly Ann, then Gervis, James, Norma, Bernita and me, then my younger sister Catherine.

Back row: Joe, Dad, Mom. Center: Gervis, Norma, James. Front: Bernita, me and Catherine.

After the evening meal we sat on the porch and Mom and Dad talked.

The porch was long, as long as the house was wide. And it was deep, about ten feet or so. After a while, my sister Waverly Ann would begin to sing. We call her "Joe", after Joe Brown the heavy weight boxer. She earned that name one night at the Evangeline Inn, a local dance Club. Waverly punched out some woman who angered her by spreading some lie. She knocked her out cold. Hence, from that day on, she was known as "Joe".

Joe began to sing a Hank Williams song. It was one that we all knew, and we soon joined in with her. The moist evening air was so dense, the sound of our song traveled unobstructed across the open fields to the neighboring hamlet. The people on the other side of the fields sat on their porches to listen to our concert. Song after song, we sang. Joe had a large collection of songs and we sang many of them during the evening. Hank Williams, who was known earlier as Luke the Drifter, had written many gospel songs. Sometime we heard a neighbor from the hamlet shout, "sing that pretty song about the old cross!" Of course he meant, "The old rugged cross". That was Dad's favorite. Joe had a strong clear voice. She could hold the notes of the song for a long time giving the tune a melody that shivered and trembled in a pleasing timbre. Her song was loud and projected and could reach the volume that carried her tune for a great distance. At the time, we had no radio, and television wasn't even around. So, we sat on the front porch and sang. Soon, the evening had passed and it was time to turn in for the night.

Mom and Dad's bedroom was in the front room. In their room was one of the two fireplaces in the house. Adjacent, was the girl's room, where Joe, Norma, and Bernita slept. Then behind the girls room was the boy's room where Gervis, James, and I slept. Gervis and James had a double bed and I had a small single bed. Everyone's mattress was made of cotton except for mine. My mattress was actually a large cotton sack filled with corn shucks on a wide board. My oldest brother, Swarn, was away in the Army. To the front of the boys room was the dinning room. It had one large table about eight feet long and four or five feet wide. At the table were four straight back chairs with cowhide seats, and two benches. A short bench was at the end of the table and one long bench on one side. Every evening we gathered at this table for our family meal. Mealtime was a time to eat and not a time for talk or noise making. A body could get a head cracked for talking or, God forbid, complain about the meal. Dinner was a tradition which we all observed. Mainly we had chicken or pork. Sometime we had smoked sausage or taso, but rarely did we have beef. We grew most of what we ate. The landlord who owned the house loaned Dad the use of a milk cow. She was a very giving cow as Dad would get at least three gallons of milk from her each day.

Next to the dining room was the kitchen. You had to step down about a foot when entering the kitchen. The house was originally slave quarters and did not have an indoor kitchen when it was built. The kitchen was added on later. In 1946, the kitchen had no cabinets. Mom had a cupboard where she kept the dishes and utensils. There was no sink or running water, and no bathroom. We had a cistern which collected rain water. A hand pump provided a means for filling buckets and tubs. Bathing was done by standing in a foot tub and washing one's self with soap and a hand towel. In the barnyard was an outhouse. However, each of the bedrooms had a chamber pot.

Mom had a typical wood burning cook stove where she prepared meals, made bread, pies, cakes, etc.

The stove and the fireplaces burned wood, and there was plenty of it. Unfortunately, it wasn't nearby. The large stand of trees, which we called "the woods", was about a mile away. But that was the way the crow flew. Dad and my older brothers drove a wagon to the woods to cut and split the firewood. James, Joe and Norma were old enough to work in the fields. Bernita and I were too young and stayed home, or when Mom worked in the fields, we were by her side playing in the cotton or the corn.

I was but a child, perhaps the age of five. Many days were spent alone in the clover field watching the clouds. All of my sisters and brothers were at school, or at work. My father worked at the saw mill during the day. Then he worked in the corn fields and the cotton fields at night. The saw mill paid my Dad ten cents an hour for ten hours work. Before daylight he milked the cow while my brothers fed the chickens, harvested the eggs, and tended to the cultivating of the vegetable gardens. My older sisters were helping my mother in the kitchen preparing breakfast and cleaning and preparing for the noon and evening meals.

Being too young to have any chores, I spent many hours in the kitchen with Mom watching her prepare meals and learning skills which I would use later in my life. At the age of five, I had many hours alone with my imagination. Not being exposed to any cultures or experiences outside of my family, my imagination was limited to domestic animals and family members. I spent long days alone, finding numerous ways to get into trouble. Chickens were always a good means of finding trouble and I always managed to find plenty of it. Once, I wanted to see if a chicken could swim. I managed to catch one and slung her into the pond in front of the house. The chicken swam just fine, and I don't think she minded the refreshing dip she had. But Mom didn't think it was a very proper thing to do to one of her laying hens. Another misfortunate bird found herself at the bottom of the outhouse because I wanted to see if she could get out. I got the belt for that one. There wasn't much I didn't try being alone in the barnyard, at the age of five…to include trying to ride the calf, tie the calf to my little red wagon, tie feathers to the cat's tail, and my favorite…putting frogs in my sister's underwear drawer. Those adventures usually got me in trouble and turned out to be not very fun after all.

One day in September of that same year, while I was still five years old, I was ushered into the first grade class room by my sister, Norma. I was to begin school that day. I would not be six years old until the following January, but my mother thought it was ok if I started the first grade a little early. Our schools didn't have kindergarten, kids just started at first grade. I sat at my desk, just as asked by the teacher. A little girl with braded pigtails sat in front of me. Haven never seen such pigtails before, I grabbed one and pulled on it. The girl screamed and the teacher swatted me on my hand with a stick. Well, I didn't think much of that, so during 10:00 a.m. recess, I left school. I didn't care much for being swatted on the hand with a stick. I went to my Nanny's house. At least, that's what I called her. Her name was Marjorie. She was one of my mother's cousins and I liked her a lot. She was always very nice to me and enjoyed caring for me while Mom worked in the fields. I knew her as my Nanny. Marjorie asked me why I was there. I said I didn't like school because the teachers were mean and that I was not going to go back. Marjorie gave me some milk and cookies then walked me home to my mother. I was swatted on the hand on my first day of school. I did not like school and I didn't like teachers. This was going to have a negative impact on me later.

Indoor Plumbing

One day, about a year later, while playing in the front yard, I saw them coming. They were huge and they moved slowly across the open pasture. As they moved closer I could hear their roar and I could feel the earth tremble beneath my feet. One was very high and it was all black. The other was smaller and white and green. They drove up right close to the fence and stopped. Two men got out of the large black truck and walked over to the gate. "Is your Daddy here, boy?" one asked. But his words could not move my attention from the big black truck. "Hello boy!" "Is anyone here?" he asked again. Then my mother came out and called at me. "Boy, get out of those men's way, they have work to do!" "Who are they Mom...what are they going to do?" "These are the men who will connect gas and water to our house" she told me. "Gas and water?" "You mean like they have at the big house at Mr. Dardeau's house?" "Yes, Mom said, and we are going to have electricity also!" "We will have a bath tub and a sink, a toilet and even hot water!" I will get a new kitchen with a sink and running water, a new gas stove and even cabinets!"

Wow! What a day this was going to be. I watched in complete awe as the men unloaded long black pipes from the huge black truck. Then one of the men set up a device called a "knuckle." It was round and had a flat face with several different size holes. The knuckle was used to cut treads at the end of the pipes for coupling to one another and make one very long pipe. The pipes had to be laid end to end to reach from the house all the way to the road on the edge of the nearby hamlet. That was the nearest gas distribution point.

It was a long way to the road. The same had to be done for the water connection. Those long pipes had to be laid and buried all the way from the house to the road.

It would take several days for the workers to connect all of those pipes and bury the line. Meanwhile, carpenters were busy building a bath room and a kitchen to the house. Workers from the electric company were planting utility pole and stringing electric lines to the house. There were men in the attic hooking up wires and dropping electric cords

down from the ceiling. They cut holes in the walls and installed electrical outlets. The old pull-down shades were replaced with venetian blinds, and a new linoleum rug was laid in the front room. The men closed off the fireplace cavity and placed a gas heater in front of it.

The old house changed. In a matter of a few weeks, the place was transformed from an 1870 slave quarter dwelling to a house with modern day twentieth century conveniences. No more long walks to the outhouse in the barnyard. No more sitting on a cold chamber pots or hauling them off the next morning. No more carrying water from the cistern. No more bathing in a foot tub. I could fill the bath tub with water and play with toy boats and submarines. This opened a whole new adventure for me. The bathtub opened a whole new avenue of creativity for me. I fashioned small boats from wood and paper and imagined fantastic scenarios of naval battles with my paper boats. Once, I was given a small metal boat powered by steam. I filled the little tank inside the boat and placed a small candle under the tank. The small flame of the candle was enough to boil the water in the tank which produces steam and propelled the tiny craft. What fun!

Chapter Two

The Movie

*S*aturday afternoon was always reserved for movies. By the age of nine, I made some friends who lived rear by and we were usually together every day. The oldest was Raymond, who was tall and skinny, and often ruled the roost. Generally we went along with whatever he said. But boys being boys, we didn't always get along too well. At that age, we were into Roy Rogers, and Gene Autry, Lash LaRue and Tim Holt. They were the famous cowboy heroes of the western movies during the 1940's and 50's. We had our fights and scuffles, and sometime we wouldn't speak to one another for days. Then somebody suggested the ole swimming hole and off we'd go and all was forgotten.

Russell was a little younger than Raymond and I, but he was tough. He hung in there with us no matter what fool notion we might have thought up, he was willing to give it a try. Russell's dad was a drunk. As soon as he had earned the price of a bottle of whiskey, he got drunk. He came home in the middle of the night and beat Russell's mother, beat Russell and his sister. More often then not, his father was picked up by the police and placed in jail until he sobered up, only to do the very same thing when he had earned the price of another bottle. Sometime it was too much for Russell to bear and he just sat with us and cried. I just let him cry because I didn't know of anything else to do. When he had cried his tears dry, we found something to do to pass the time. We were masters at building bows and arrows, or sling shots. We had a tree called a China ball tree which made hard green berries. These berries were about three eights to one half inch in diameter. There was also a cane of some

11

sort; I don't know what it was called. But this cane grew to about one and a quarter inch in diameter, and had a soft core which was exactly the same size as the berries of the china ball tree. The canes were cut about eight to ten inches in length. The core was pushed out with a plunger made out of a broom handle. Placing a berry at both ends of this cane and pushing one of the berries through the cane with the plunger created pressure in the cane and shot the other berry out of the cane at great velocity, creating a weapon of war. We had china ball wars all the time. If the cane was long enough, you could put three or four berries in the chamber and have an automatic repeater. Hot dog, that was the style. When your opponent was reloading, you could pop him two or three times. Yeah!

But Saturday afternoon was for movie going, and this particular Saturday, I was very anxious to get to the movie. The film had been advertised for two weeks and I couldn't wait to get to the theatre. The movie was "The Bridges at Toko-Ri®". The film was about Navy Jet Fighters attacking bridges in North Korea. I loved to see any film of military war planes, but this was Navy Fighters, and the actor was William Holden. At the age of nine, I found a dream, a dream to fly in jet fighters and discover what was on the other side of the clouds. I loved the movies, and I especially loved to watch those jets fly so gracefully through the clouds. I had no idea about how movies were made; they were fascinating to me and I was mesmerized by their magic. I often wondered what it was like to fly in those jets through the open sky, free as a bird; I could only dream of someday being in one of those planes, flying to the other side of the clouds. How I wished that I could fly in those jets and make movies of jets flying through the clouds. I wanted to learn about making movies; I dreamed of being a motion picture cameraman, flying through the clear blue sky, free as a bird.

The movie came and went, and while it was forgotten by most people, it lingered in my mind. During the hot summer months of my later years while at the age of twelve, thirteen, and fourteen, Raymond, Russell and I were in the cotton fields earning money for the coming fall school year. I earned enough money to buy several pairs of blue jeans and cotton shirts to wear to school. We earned two cents a pound for the cotton we picked each day. The day began when mom woke me at about three in the morning. I dressed in jeans and a tee shirt, then a long sleeve flannel shirt over the tee shirt. The air at three in the morning was cold, and the grass and fields were covered with dew from the previous evening. I walked across the field in front of the house to the road where I met Russell and Raymond. We exchanged greetings and complained about the cold air and waited for the man. Soon a farmer came by in his truck to take us to his cotton fields. I hated getting up so early and walking out into the cold air just to go do something I disliked even more…picking cotton. There simply was no other way to earn money. The town of Ville Platte where I lived had no industry. It was a small town in the center of an agrarian community. Cotton and other harvesting was the only employment.

After a thirty to forty minute ride, we arrived at the farmer's cotton field and were handed picking sacks. These sacks were large enough to hold several pounds of cotton. When we entered the fields, it was not yet daylight. The cotton was wet from the dew, and that meant that you picked the fastest before the sun came up and dried the cotton. The wet cotton weighed more than when it was dry. One could make more money in the early damp morning than in the dry hot midday. The dark morning air was cold. The long sleeve flannel shirt felt warm in the cold wet air. After the sun came up, the long sleeves came off, and we were in tee shirts for the rest of the day. The cotton bowls were wide open and the cotton was fluffed out. The fast picking sometime meant that on occasions you got stung by the sharp pointed ends of the dried bowl. This was very painful, and at the end of the day your fingers and hands were rubbed raw by the spiny cotton bowls.

At about noon, the farmer drove his truck into the field where we were picking and took in the first weigh-in of the day. He had a log where he recorded our cotton weight. After the weigh-in, he drove us to the house for lunch. The farmer's wife had prepared a meal for all of us. Other than we three boys, there may have been as many as twelve to fifteen other pickers in the group. So the woman had prepared a very large amount of food.

Sometime the other pickers were entire families father and mother and four or five children of all ages. The father pushed the children and when they didn't pick fast enough he switched them across the back with whip like branch from a willow tree. Often he would yell at them and threaten them with the switch. They were always black families and they had to wait to eat until the white pickers had eaten. Most of the meals were of pork or chicken…animals that the farmer raised on his farm. We rarely had beef or smoked meat. But it usually was good food. Normally, we returned to the field at about 2:30 pm to avoid the scorching hot sun of mid-day. While back in the field, the heat of the day caused huge white clouds to form. Occasionally, I granted myself the luxury of stealing a glimpse at a cloud formation to see if I could imagine a face or an image, and I wondered what clouds look like from the other side. The moment lasted for only a second, but for me it was like an eternity. Some days the sky was perfectly clear. Not a cloud to be seen. I felt cheated. Where were my clouds? This was to be a long day for sure. We picked cotton until it was too dark to see the cotton bowls. The farmer recorded the final weigh-in, then, paid us two cents per pound for cotton we picked, and return us to the side of the road where he picked us up, and we walked home. When I got home, I gave mom the money I had earned that day. I ate a quick supper and went straight to bed.

The very next day, and the many days that followed until September, when we again entered school, every day was the same. Meet the farmer's truck early in the morning, pick cotton all day, and return home to go directly to bed.

Everyday when I was in the fields, I watched the sky for clouds. From the early morning hours of darkness to the time sun rose to warm the fields, I watched the skies. Generally around 10:00 am when the air began to warm and get heavy, the clouds began to form. First, low on the horizon and far away, then closer…and closer. Then, they were directly overhead. I could see the massive summer clouds forming and moving across the bright blue sky. I watched them move into intricate shapes forming faces and figures…And I could not forget the scenes in the movie of the Navy jets flying through and above the clouds…and I wondered, what clouds look like on the other side. I was haunted by the scenes of the movie. Many nights I dreamed myself to sleep thinking about those Navy planes as they flew so graciously across the sky in seemingly effortless movements. Oh how I envied those heroic men as they defiantly flew their planes into the heavily guarded bridges they had been ordered to destroy. I could not shake the desire to do what they were doing. I wondered about the magic of the movies and how movies were created. I wondered.

Chapter Three

The Power
of
Failure

*N*ot all of our summers were spent in the cotton fields. We did have lots of time for having fun. Before the town swimming pool was built, we walked to swimming holes. One hole in particular that was always available for a cool dip during the hot summer days was known as the "yellow hole" because the water was yellow. It was a natural spring that had developed in a sulfur pit. The sulfur turned the water yellow. The hole wasn't very big and not too deep. But, it provided a pastime for the long hot summer days. The yellow hole served as our swimming hole. That is until the irrigation pumps began to run.

Rice was a popular crop in Louisiana when I was growing up, and there were many rice fields everywhere. Growing rice requires a large amount of water and very flat land. Louisiana is well suited for rice crops because the land is indeed flat and the water table was very high, meaning that a large amount of water was available near the surface of the ground. The water was pumped out using huge pumps. It emerged from the ground through large pipes ten inches in diameter aimed upward at a 45 degree angle and rose eight to ten feet into the air. The force of water hitting the ground eventually created a large pond that reached depths of twelve to twenty feet. The bottom of the pond had a natural gravel layer which prevented mud from building and the water remained crystal clear and cold.

Water flowed from the pump pond to the rice fields by way of canals. It sometime had to travel hundreds and thousands of yards to reach the fields. In order to prevent erosion of the canal walls and lose the water, farmers dug relief ponds every so many thousand feet. The relief ponds slowed the flow of water and removed the pressure on the canal walls. The pump ponds and the relief ponds were fun places to be on long hot summer days. We used scrap lumber to build diving platforms on the edge of the ponds. The farmers did not like us swimming in the pump ponds mainly because of the danger created by fast moving water. But that never stopped us from going in there. Yes, we got caught on occasions, and the farmer ran us off cursing and yelling obscenities, but that just encourage us to come back later. In Louisiana, it is rather difficult to separate a boy and a swimming hole. The rice fields had to be flooded for several months, and as a result, we had available swimming water for a long time.

Russell and I were too young to go off with my brothers and the other older fellows to the pump ponds. We were just too small and could not swim that well. One day when the older boys went off to the ponds, Russell and I went into the rice fields behind our house. The water was only about eighteen inches deep, and we could do the great American mud crawl through the rice field. The water was nice and warm from the sun and it felt good. So, we stripped down to our birthday suits and began to crawl. We didn't notice at first, but the Landlord was making his rounds of the fields on horseback. When we spotted him, we snuggled down low on the bottom of the rice paddy. A blind man could have seen us. Our white little butts shinning in the noonday sun could have been seen from the moon. Well, the landlord ordered us out of his field and didn't let us put our clothes back on, and walked us back to my house where we both got a switching from my mom.

The Hand-Me-Down Bicycle

In the year 1954, Dad got a job at the local Conoco Gas plant. My mother's brother was employed there and helped Dad get hired. Dad was hired as a 'roustabout'. That is what they called a "Jack of all trades...and a master of none". But Dad was quite the master. He didn't have much education... only to the eight grade but he knew enough arithmetic to know when or if the company had cheated him on his paycheck. Dad could fix anything. He had an inventor's mind. When we grew a lawn in front of the house, he had only an old push mower someone gave him. He rebuilt the mower then figured out how to put a gasoline engine on it. Later he purchased an electric mower and put the engine on his bike. I believe he had the first "Moped" ever.

The plant was about six or seven miles from town and Dad had no means of transportation. He convinced our local Western Auto store manager to extend him credit on the purchase of a bicycle. The price of the bike was $20.00. Dad promised to pay $2.00 every paycheck, which came about every fifteen days, until the debt was paid. The bike was a Western Auto Western Flyer. It was beautiful. It was bright red with white stripes on the fenders and body. It was a twenty eight inch with heavy duty tires for comfortable riding.

Dad rode his bike to the corner of North Corel and Main streets, about two miles from home, where he met other workers with a car and rode to work with them. The bike was safely padlocked and parked behind the barber shop. In the evening after work he rode his bike back home.

Some years later, Dad and Mom had saved up enough money to put a good down payment on a used car. They chose a grey 1946 Ford Coupe. It was a handsome little car with a three gear lever shift on the steering column. Soon after my parents bought their first car is when we took our first trip. We visited his brother, Uncle Wills and Aunt Ida in Port Arthur, Texas. My, this was a long trip, further than I had ever been away from home. It took us the better part of four hours to get there, leaving at 4:00 am.

The view from atop of the Port Arthur Bridge across the Neches River was spectacular. The bridge rose to 177 feet above the river. But to me it might as well have been a thousand feet high. Driving over that bridge gave me my first inclination as to how exciting flying would be.

With the advent of having motorized transportation, Dad passed the bicycle down to us. First Gervis and James learned to ride, then Norma and Bernita. The bike was handed down to everyone and when it finally was passed to me, it was no longer a beautiful red bike with white stripes, but green, heavily layered with paint and dented fenders and badly worn tires. But, it was mine. I had a miserable time trying to learn to ride that darn bike. I was all alone; none of my siblings were around to help me. The bike was a twenty eight inch and I was very short. Finally, one day I figured out a way to get on the bike. I placed some apple crates next to the bike. I climbed on…and …Eureka! I was riding. I rode the bike to the road at the edge of town then reached the paved streets and rode and rode. I didn't ever want to get off. Finally it was getting dark and I decided to head for home. I was so excited that I could ride a bike, and the bike that had passed through all of my brothers and sisters was now mine. I couldn't wait for the next morning to come so I could ride my bike again. But the next morning proved not to be as exciting as I thought. All the riding I did the day before caused noticeable pain in my posterior and it was a few days later that I again rode my ugly green bike.

Ville Platte gets a cement swimming hole!

Then, the unbelievable happened. The city opened a swimming pool less than a mile from where we lived, a permanent swimming hole where no one told us to get out or prevented us from entering. However, the cost for going into the pool was ten cents. Sometime, we didn't have a dime to pay to get in. And therein laid another challenge, how to sneak into the pool and not get caught. We devised several ingenious ways of sneaking in. One of our favorites was very simple. We collected enough money for one person to pay to get in. A large safety pen with a number on it, attached to the swim suit, signified to the managers that the person had paid the admission. That person then would meet the rest of us by the fence, out of sight of the manager and passed the pen through the fence until we had all entered the pool, seemingly legal.

Summer was also for fishing

Summer time meant fishing time and we loved to fish. Too bad for us, we didn't have any good fishing holes like swimming holes and the best place for fishing was at Chicot (pronounced shee-co) State park, about fifteen miles from Ville Platte. The park was very well organized with clean campsites, picnic tables and toilet facilities and was a draw for picnickers, campers, boating and fishing. One could catch large mouth bass, crappie, catfish and lots of other fun fish to catch. The problem was getting there. Raymond suggested that we walk. "Walk?" "Walk to the State Park?" "Are you nuts?" I said. "We can't walk to the park, it's too far!"

"We can cut through the woods, shorting the trip by at least seven miles." "When we reach the highway we can hitch hike the rest of the way to the park."

It sounded reasonable to me, but Russell and Jimmy were a little uneasy about cutting through the woods. "What if we get lost in the woods?" Russell asked. "We may not find our way back." "I don't think my mom will let me go," Jimmy said. "What do you mean…let you go?" "You don't ask her, you just go!" "I'm scared!" Jimmy said. "I'm going home!"

Russell didn't want to go either. So, Raymond and I headed across the woods towards the highway that would take us to Chicot State Park and a grand day of fishing.

After what seemed to be an endless day of walking, about four hours, we reached the road to the park and began hitch hiking. "Here comes a car." Raymond said. He stuck out his thumb in a hitch hiking fashion, and the car slowed to a stop. It was Archile Vidrine, one of the local high school seniors and some friends. "Where are you boys going?" Archie asked. "We are headed for Chicot State Park." Raymond answered. "On foot?" Archie asked. "You guys are crazy!" "Get in the car!" he shouted. Then he drove off towards the park. Archie told us that he and his friends were going to be at the park for the day and that we should meet them at the car around five o'clock. Raymond and I didn't have money to rent a boat which cost $1.00 for the day, so we had to fish from the bank of the lake. We didn't catch much fish and didn't have much to show for a tiring and exhausting day. Archie brought us home and I was very glad to be home after that day.

Catfish stew, or catfish étouffée, fish cooked in a tomato sauce, one of my favorites, is a plentiful commodity in Louisiana and the fish are easily caught in roots of trees on the edge of the bayou. It is also one of the most dangerous means of catfishing. Water moccasins, loggerhead turtles and alligators are prevalent in these waters and they do not like to be disturbed. This method of catching fish is successful during the months of July and August when the

21

water level in the bayou is low and the roots of trees are most exposed. The ole catfish worm their way under the tree roots for a cool afternoon nap in the shade away from the hot summer sun. During the peak of the day, between 1:00 to 3:00 pm is the best time to catch the catfish sleeping. The trick is rather simple; enter the water downstream from the area where there may be a sleeping big 'cat' and slowly approach the tree roots being careful not to disturb the water. Once at the roots, use both hands to feel under the surface for the sleeping fish. Gently, and ever-so-slowly move along the body until the head is reached. Very softly, open the fish's gill with easy finger movement and ease the big boy out from under the roots and with one swift lurch, throw the catfish up on the bank. There, you have catfish étouffée coming up!

Another favorite way we fished was setting trot lines. This type of fishing was mainly done at night.

My cousin Frank and I were close to the same age and grew up together in Ville Platte during the 1940s and 50s.

Frank and I hunted, mostly ducks, rabbits and squirrels. We fished also, but mostly when his dad or older brother, Max took us. Uncle Wilson, Frank's Dad, loved to fish and camp out at the lake. Frank had the use of his father's pickup truck; although he was not of legal driving age. Frank and I planned a fishing trip on Saturday evening in October at Chicot State Park. The weather was clear, a bit cool and a little windy. Friday afternoon we went to the local chicken processing plant to get fresh bait. The best bait for catfish is chicken livers or intestine which was given free.

One of the neighbors said that we would not be very successful that Saturday because the weather was going to turn cold with a front passing through. "It's gonna be a cold North wind tonight yeah" he told us. "Catfish don't bit nut'en when the wind blows from the North". "You'd be waisen yo' time" he said. Uncle Wilson, who was part Choctaw Indian said, "don't pay any mind to that ole fool, he ain't neva catch any fish in his life, him"!

This was the first time that Frank and I would go fishing overnight without his father or Max. With the boat, tent, and fishing tackle loaded in the back of the pickup, we were on our way for an exciting night of catfishing on the lake at Chicot SP.

We pitched the tent and prepared the boat and the trot lines. A trot line is a heavy cotton string about forty feet long with a hook places about every twelve inches. The line is strung across the channel and anchored at both ends to trees or shrubs. We set fourteen lines that afternoon before dark but did not bait the hooks right away, setting the bait in the afternoon before the sun set would attract smaller unwanted fish, turtles, or worse, snakes.

As the day was ending and the sun began to disappear behind the trees, the temperature dropped very quickly. The approaching cold front changed the weather conditions as the North wind whistled through the tall pine trees. When darkness fell, it was time to bait our hooks and start fishing.

Frank packed everything we needed for our catfish étouffée cooked over an open fire. He had a cast iron pot with two inch long feet and another pot for steaming rice, plus all of the ingredients for that wonderful tomato base sauce. All we needed was fish.

As soon as the last of the trot lines were baited, which took over an hour, we returned to the first line to harvest our catch. It was amazing; almost every hook had a fish weighing a pound or more. As we collected the fish, we re-baited the hooks and returned the line to the water. When all the lines were serviced it was past nine o'clock and we had filled one of our two ice chests. We returned to the campsite, cleaned a few fish and Frank made our supper. Cooking fish over an open fire was a new experience for me and my mouth watered with anticipation as I watched the tomato and onion sauce bubble slowly in the pot. Not being experienced in the culinary arts as Frank was, I felt as useless as a fifth wheel. Frank suggested I could make myself useful by gathering up more fire wood; as he informed me that it would be a long night.

After we had eaten our gourmet delight and stretched out for a moment, it was time to run the lines. The hour was approaching midnight and the North wind continued to howl through the darkened forest. Our lines were heavy with dangling fish as we pulled in line after line. When we finished the midnight run, we had filled both of the large ice chests. Frank turned to me with a worrisome look on his face. "We have too much fish" he shouted. "We still have lines in the water and we will probably have just as many in an hour"! "We will have to take this fish home and have our folks clean them and put them away, while we come back here and pull in our lines"! "Okay", I answered, "but my dad will not be happy about this, he hates fish"!

When we reached the house, I ran in shouting for everyone to wake up. Dad came running out of his bedroom wearing nothing but his underwear and waving a shotgun. "What the Sam Hell is going on" he yelled. "Dad", I said, Frank and I have caught too many fish and we run out of space to hold them". "We will have to leave these with you and Mom and Uncle Wilson and Aunt Panny to clean while we go back to the lake to pull in our lines". "We need the ice chests to bring back the fish that are on the lines now". "What the hell are we going to do with so much fish"? Dad asked. "Eat them"! I said.

The summer passed very quickly, and too soon we were back in class for a long dreary nine months of school. The year 1959 became very significant to me. It was the year I turned sixteen. It was the year that I began to feel the power of failure. School was not going well for me. It wasn't that I couldn't learn; it was because I didn't want to do the work required to learn. Ever since my first grade teacher swatted me on the hand on my first day of school, I hated school. I convinced myself that I didn't like school and I didn't need it. As the end of the school year drew closer, my grades fell lower and lower. My disparity and lack of interest in school grew with each failure. I completely lost all confidence in my ability to do anything and had accepted my fate of being a dead failure. To fail high school at such a young age, and being able to accept my fate, meant only that failure could come much easier next time, and be easier to accept. The power of failure consumed me and I was doomed to join the ranks of the unsuccessful. I became a high school dropout. I experienced the power of failure, and it didn't feel good.

That summer I was told by a very angry and disappointed father that I was to find a job and begin to pay my way while living under his roof. He further stated that he was not going to have a lazy good-for-nothing bum living in his house. And he was right. I had no right living off of him. However wanting a job and getting a job were two different things. The town of Ville Platte had no industry. Most people who had jobs worked off shore on oil rigs. I had no such skills, no abilities. I had no marketable skills. I had no self-confidence. I was a failure, a high school dropout and nothing more. I was destined to be a liability of the state. I was uneducated and unemployable. I had placed myself into the worst possible situation. Haven failed myself, I also failed my father who held great hope for me to be a success. The shame would be with me for many years.

The local Louisiana National Guard was to be my salvation. The Guard was looking for new recruits, and they didn't look very closely to the age of their young prospects. Several of the boys in my age group were members of the Guard and they spoke well of the organization. They were required to attend one monthly meeting and two weeks of summer camp. For this, they were paid a monthly salary. So I thought I would give it a try. I reported to Fort Jackson, South Carolina for basic training that September.

Chapter Four

I'm in the Army Now!

I had failed the tenth grade and dropped out of high school. Any hope of ever becoming a motion picture cameraman and flying in jets had just slipped away out of reach. I had to hang my dream on a cloud. Just like the clouds, my dream was empty of substance. I could no more get off the ground than I could walk on a cloud. A dream was all it was. A dream without goals is merely a wish, and wishes do not come true. I later learned, that to be successful, one must work hard and be willing to sacrifice. All that is worthy of having has to be earned. I learned this later in my life. Now, I had something else I had to do. "I was in the Army!"

When the bus arrived at the Reception Center at Fort Jackson, we were ordered off the bus by screaming Drill Sergeants barking at us like mad dogs. Not one moment of silence. No matter how fast we moved it wasn't fast enough. We were stupid scumbags, illegitimate excuses for human beings. We were rushed through IQ testing, through the quartermaster store for uniform fitting, through medical examination, immunization, haircuts, through supply for bedding, and it went on and on. I thought, "This is the American Army, surely they won't kill me today!" It was almost ten o'clock when we were told to get undressed and go to bed. The lights went out, and I heard Taps for the first time. When the last note of the trumpet had ended, sobbing was heard in the distant space of the darkened barracks. Then I realized that I was not the only one who needed to cry. I turned my face into my pillow and began to weep. How was I ever going to get through this? I was a mere boy, sixteen years old, who had never been away from home alone except to visit my grandmother in Mamou, only fourteen miles from Ville Platte. This was not going to be a hike in the woods with Raymond and Russell, or a trip to the forbidden swim hole…I was in the Army! I managed to cry myself to sleep, and all too soon, the next morning came.

It was only 3:00 a.m. and this Drill Sergeant was screaming at the top of his lungs and beating on beds, rolling mattresses on the floor with the occupants still in them. **"Get up you good-for-nothing scumbags, get out of those racks, hit the floor and stand at attention at the head of your bunk and count off!!"** My stomach was growling with hunger and my knees were shaking so badly I could hardly stand. I could smell the mess hall next door. I don't know what they were cooking, but it smelled like Mom's meatball stew…and I got even hungrier. The Drill Sergeant rushed us out of the barracks and in to the company street for formation. He made a headcount to make sure that everyone was present and accounted for. We were then marched to the mess hall for breakfast.

My platoon Drill Sergeant was a little guy. I was small, only five feet six inches, but he was even shorter. That didn't change the fact that he was as mean as a rattlesnake and stern as a mule and you didn't want to mess with him. He had been through World War II and the Korean War and had a chest full of ribbons and medals. When he marched us as a platoon he could walk forward, backwards and sideways and never miss a step. He was incredible to watch…like a ballet. He noticed that I was very young, younger than the other troops and he didn't believe that I was seventeen years old. I was so afraid that he would report me for having a fraudulent enlistment and send me home. I couldn't go back home. I had to finish this or I would never have the courage to try anything ever again in my life. I still had a dream of someday reaching the clouds still I didn't know how I was going to do it. I knew that I could not fail again. If I could not make it through Army Basic Training I was not ever going to succeed at anything.

At night while others were asleep I would be in the latrine polishing my boots and studying my General Orders and other materials we had to memorize and be able to recite at a moments notice. We had eleven General Orders, six articles of the Code of Conduct, our serial numbers which consisted of nine digits just like our social security numbers and a rifle serial number with seven digits. All of this we had to memorize and recite. I would polish boots and study for two hours after the lights went out at ten pm.

Eight weeks passed by quickly and it was graduation day. I was graduating from Army basic training. I felt proud. I wanted my mother to see me. I wanted her to know that even though I had failed high school, perhaps I could succeed at something else. I wanted her to see me in my uniform, the way it fit all snug and trim. I was hard as a rock. And no wonder, basic training was tough. We were up at 4:30 every morning at First call.   We had fifteen minutes to shower, shave get dressed, and be out in the company street for formation and reveille. Immediately following reveille, we were marched to the parade field for morning calisthenics. It was the daily dozen. Twelve exercises, twelve repetitions of each. Push-ups, sit-ups, jumping jacks, deep knee bends, were all exercises to build a strong body. After exercises, we were marched back to the company area for breakfast. Eggs to order, bacon and sausage, potatoes, toast, Oatmeal, orange juice, milk all made for a good hardy breakfast. And we had five minutes to get it down and out of the mess hall. Then, the tough day began.

All of the training companies were on Tanker Hill. They called it that because that is where the huge water tanks were. Every morning we marched down Tanker Hill to the training areas. The road to the training areas was not paved. It was just a sandy dirt road, and your feet sunk about six inches into the loose sand. This made it even more difficult to walk and the training areas were a good distance away. The days in the South Carolina weather were steaming hot. Our uniforms had long sleeves with the shirts buttoned all the way to the neck. The combat boots that had been spit-shined to a mirror finish the night before were heavy and stiff. Many of the soldiers had blisters on their blisters. But that mattered not. This was basic training and no place for wimps. At noon, our food was delivered by truck at the training site. We carried mess kits in our back-packs, along with a shelter half, tent poles and pegs, an entrenching tool, an extra pair of underwear and socks, soap, toothbrush, tooth powder, and a few personal items. In all the back pack weighed about sixty-five pounds.

The meals were generally pretty good. Most of the men did not like vegetables much, and I did. So I always had plenty to eat. One day the cooks served us spaghetti and meat sauce. One of the guys liked the meal so much; he went back to the serving line for seconds. That was a big mistake. It was very much like the scene in Oliver Twist, when the sergeant yelled out "More"? "You want more"? "I'll give you more"! The sergeant said, and he loaded the man's mess kit with what must have been a pound of spaghetti. I almost got sick just watching him try to eat it all.

At the end of the training day we marched back to the company area. Walking up Tanker Hill was the toughest part of basic training. The hill was almost a 45 degree climb, in that loose sand, and we had to maintain perfect cadence and remain in step. The Drill Sergeant had several little songs he sang to help us stay in step. First he started with a count…"Hut to your left, your left, your left right left". Each time he said "left" our left foot was hitting the ground. When he said "right" our right foot hit. Then, he sang his little song…"ain't no use at looking down…ain't no discharge on the ground"! Then he said, "sound off!" And we would sing out, "One Two" "Sound off!" "Three Four!" "Bring it on down!" "One Two Three Four, One Two Three Four!" His little songs were quite cute sometime, and they helped to pass the time and make the walk more enjoyable.

I had gained several pounds in eight weeks and became very strong. We had several competitions during the eight week course of basic training. This was to help build moral and development confidence. I had won the push-up and pull-up contests. I was in great shape. I wanted my mother to feel proud. Finally, I had accomplished something. Even though I was compelled to do well by the Drill Sergeants, I had completed Basic Army Training. I personally experienced the taste of success and it felt good.

I was ordered directly to Fort Leonard Wood, Missouri to begin Combat Engineer training. I didn't understand why I had to go there at that time, when the other basic training graduates were getting two week leaves. I later found out that in five weeks the last Special Warfare Training group at Fort Leonard Wood was going to start. I was specifically selected for this training because of the skills I demonstrated in basic training. I was a good soldier, an expert rifleman with a lot of discipline. It was the opinion of the sergeants in basic training that I was well suited for Special Warfare Training. Although this was strictly a volunteer program, the Army was recruiting men to the group. If someone did not want to participate in the training, they could be dismissed. But once the training started, it was very difficult to drop out, and the Army did not look upon dropouts in a favorable manner. Those who dropped, and there were many, were branded as quitters and did not have a very successful career. The training group started with one hundred and fifty trainees on November 20, 1959 and graduated thirty five Special Warfare Combatants on March 2, 1960. The failure rate for this training was very high because the training was very tough. During the daylight hours we mostly attended lectures. At night, we practiced the lessons we had learned earlier. We spent hours in the dark forest practicing and learning to be special combatants. Most of the objectives were to gather intelligence on the enemy, or to sabotage the units in some way. I lay quietly in the tall grass motionless for many hours waiting for the right moment to advance towards my objective.

The final week of training was to demonstrate our skills and prove that we were ready to serve as Special Warfare Combatants. We were issued a bayonet, a book of matches, six feet of string, and a compass and map and were taken out into the training area at night by truck. Each time the truck stopped, one of us was released and the truck moved on. My instructions were to locate a company of basic trainees and gather intelligence. I was given only very brief information as to their location. The exercise was to take three days. I was captured on the second day and placed in a prisoner of war camp, interrogated and humiliated and mentally tortured for days. Then finally it was over. I had completed the course.

The fact that I had failed high school seemed relatively unimportant now. I was barely seventeen years old and one of America's best trained soldiers in a very elite cadre of men. We were the ones who had been chosen to be tested, and the ones who passed.

The years passed quickly and in 1962 I was in Okinawa assigned to a Hawk Missile unit. The Hawk is an anti-aircraft ground to air missile. Every year, each missile battalion must go to the range, fire missiles and qualify as an air defensive unit. We were at the range firing missiles at practice drowns when I saw a soldier operating a very strange machine. The machine was about the size of a shoe box, round at one end, but square at the other. The strange looking box had round tubes sticking out of it. It was mounted on top of a tripod and the man looked into it as if to view something.

I approached this man and inquisitively and politely ask him what kind of machine that was that he was operating. "It's a motion picture camera" he replied. "A motion picture camera???" I asked. "Yes", he said, I am a Motion Picture Cameraman". I could not believe what I was hearing. "You mean, you make movies for the Army…that is your job in the Army"? "Yes, he said, I am filming you guys firing those missiles". "wow" I screamed…"How do I get to do that"? I asked him. "You go to school" he said. I turned and walked away in disbelief. I looked up at the sky. The clouds were high and thick. The sun was behind them and the golden light had formed a bright silver and gold lining behind the largest and highest…and again I yearned to see what clouds looked like on the other side. "Could this be real?" I asked, "Could I really become a motion picture cameraman simply by going to school?"

Soon after the training at the missile range was over, I visited my unit's career counselor to inquire about Motion Picture school. He said that I could go to this school but that I would have to re-enlist in the Army for at least three years. Several weeks went by, then finally I was informed of my acceptance to Motion Picture School. I was so excited I could hardly keep from screaming. This was the happiest days of my life. The dream of becoming a motion picture cameraman was soon to be a reality. I would lay awake at night finding it hard to believe that it was actually true. My excitement grew with each passing day in anticipation of the coming event. The days could not pass quickly enough. The plane carrying me back to the United States seemed to be dragging. I could hardly wait to begin school.

Motion Picture school was fourteen weeks long and my experience at Fort Monmouth, New Jersey was short and brief. My friends and I took a trip to New York for a weekend. That trip was just long enough to tell me that I liked nothing about New York and did not care to return.

One of the most memorable events of Fort Monmouth, and motion picture school was when we were assigned to an infantry company on bivouac at Fort Dix, New Jersey. We were assigned to this infantry company to film simulated combat action. While we were filming night maneuvers, we discovered a forest fire apparently started by some of our practice fire. We hurried to film the fire and the firefighters, when we stumbled upon a man selling moonshine. Well, as the evening progressed, we stumbled upon more and more of this moonshine and our adventure grew more interesting. We filmed some wonderful stuff on fire fighting, then, returned to the infantry company bivouac to settle in for the evening. It was past 1:00 a.m. when we returned. George Gentry tripped over the Company Commander's bunk as he walked into the tent, and later that night, Tommy Pool relieved his bladder on the oil heating stove which steamed the tent with a stench of burnt urine. Needless to say, we were asked to leave the very next morning.

Motion picture training was very challenging for me. I had not graduated from high school and a lot of the elements of photography required good math skills. The proper exposure in photography is dealing with shutter speeds and F stops. The shutter speed determines how fast the photo is taken, and the F stop determines how much light is allowed through the lens in a given time. It can be very complicated at times. But I was learning new mathematical skills and the instructors were very through and excellent teachers. I hadn't learned well in high school because the math problems were very abstract and without values. Shutter speeds and F stops had definite meaning and were more easily understood.

Mostly, the training involved how to properly operate the camera, and learning how to properly compose a scene. The proper operation of the camera was most important. We had simple scripts to follow at first, then, the scenes became more complex. At the end of every three weeks of training were phase test to record levels and degree of learning.

I completed the course and I graduated. This was the third major accomplishment since I had failed the tenth grade and dropped out of high school. I successfully completed Army basic training, Special Warfare Training, and now I was graduating from motion picture school. How cool was that? I had been dreaming of making movies since I was nine years old, when I thought movies were magic. Now, I would be making magic. I had finally achieved one of my goals. Maybe someday I could see the other side of the clouds! Maybe!

After graduating from Motion Picture Photography School, I was ordered to Germany, and assigned to the 97th Signal Battalion at Boeblingen, Germany. I reported on July 25, 1963 and would be there for three years. The photo platoon had a really good bunch of guys. Most of them had a wonderful since of humor and they were just a lot of fun to be with. Our platoon sergeant was a leftover from the Korean War and World War II. A real wet rag who we called 'Mother', because he 'mothered' us so. His second in command, a sergeant Spencer, was a real wash-out. He had been passed-over for promotion so many times, it was sad. He had been an E-5 as long as I had been alive and he would never be promoted to E-6. But, the guys in the platoon were great. The photo platoon sponsored an orphanage in the local community. Throughout the year, the guys raised money for this orphanage. They raised money selling cakes and cookies some of the wives made. The Enlisted club contributed a lot of money made from slot machines and from hamburger sales. A lot of people helped to raise the funds to help these orphans.

In the summer, around the end of May, orphans from all over Germany were bused in to this local orphan summer camp near the base. It was a magnificent event to see all these kids coming into the camp to enjoy two weeks of vacation and fun. And it was all funded by us, the photo platoon. The following May1964, when the orphans were to arrive, we discovered that our new platoon sergeant had invited the company commander, the battalion commander, the Sergeant major. This was to be nothing but a big political white wash for our new platoon sergeant. Many of the platoon members just said "shove it", "we're not going!" And very few of the platoon members did attend the ceremony that we had been looking forward to for so long.

Instead, my friend Jim Robinson and I went to the swimming pool in Boeblingon, the near by town. We spent the day at the pool, mostly looking at the girls, drinking a beer or two, eating a Bratwurst. But I spent a lot of time lying on my back looking at the clouds, and wondering what clouds look like from the other side. About 4:00 p.m., Jim said, "let's take a walk and look at the girls". So, we did. Our walk took us near to the dressing rooms. As we passed, I saw a young girl combing her wet hair as she looked in the mirror. I stopped for a glance, then, walked on. Suddenly I stopped as if someone or something hit me in the head with a baseball bat. "Go Back Dummy" I heard a voice scream in my head. I went back. Fortunately, she was still there. I watched her. Then, she noticed that I was watching her. She smiled at me. I froze. I didn't know what I was going to say, and to this day, I don't know what I said, but we had a date to meet at the pool the very next day.

The next day, I was at the pool, at the place which we had agreed to meet. I was so nervous; I was so filled with anticipation. I could not remember what she looked like. "I couldn't even remember her name"! "Did she tell me her name"? I didn't know. "Oh my God, I don't know her name"! "What does she look like"? "I don't know"! "How will I know her"? A young girl was approaching. "Is that her"? "No, she… she has different eyes"! The girl smiled at me. "No, that's not her…her smile is different"! I started pacing up and down. "What if she doesn't come"? "What if she forgot"? I had arrived early, so, perhaps she wasn't late. Maybe her bus had been delayed. Then, I saw her. There she was, with that smile I had seen in the mirror the day before, and suddenly I remembered…her name was Irmtraut. Irmtraut Mayer. Her first name was going to be difficult to deal with. She told me her friends call her "Emmy". So I changed "Emmy" to "Amy". This was the girl I would marry and with whom I would spend the rest of my life.

Chapter Five

Vietnam

We met on Saturday, May 29, and we were married on Friday, December 11, 1964. Our home was a one room apartment, with a small kitchen across the hall. The house was in the little picturesque town of Schoenaich. We shared a bathroom with the family from whom we rented. It was small, but then it was all that we needed at the time. The little apartment was just a place to store some clothing and a place to sleep. Later, a larger apartment upstairs, with a private bath became available. Just in the nick of time too, because on May fourteenth, we were no longer alone with each other. Sherry Ann was born at 8:15 a.m. on that day.

I traveled very often while I was with the 97th Signal Battalion. I didn't like leaving my wife and daughter alone, but I had no choice, those were some of the sacrifices we must make in order to achieve our goals. I wanted to grow in the Army and be the best I could be. Besides, Amy's mother lived only a few kilometers away, and the family who owned the house we lived in were very good people. So, I didn't have many concerns. I was having the best time of my life as a motion picture cameraman. I was traveling all over Germany filming hometown news interviews with the troops, filming tank battle exercises and other war games. I even got to fly in a small observer plane to shoot some aerials of troop maneuvers. It was a really small plane, not like a Navy jet. But it was fun. I could only dream what it would be like to fly in a Navy jet filming other jets as they gracefully flew through the clear blue sky. But that was only a dream.

I traveled with the same people most of the time. My friend Jim Robinson, Jim was from Colorado, and Louis

Marcellus. Louis was an Italian-Canadian, we called 'Luigi Antonio Josepi Wheelbarrel Marcellus. Luigi was as wide as he was tall, but strong as an ox. He had a heart of gold. He loved people but was quiet as a mouse. The three of us traveled throughout West Germany, and even into Italy and France, Denmark, and once Jim went to Norway.

Jim was younger than I, very well educated and loved to read. He always had his head in a book. He was tall and lanky and walked with gait, like an unsophisticated hillbilly. But he was far from that. He was well versed in philosophy and could discuss an issue in modern art, or interpret the emotion of progressive jazz. He favored Thelonious Monk over Country or Rock music. Jim hounded me for not having finished high school. He suggested I go to the Education Center and complete a GED program. I told him that I didn't have time, I had to travel in my job and I just didn't have time to do it. Finally, he pointed out the fact that by not having a high school education, I was limiting myself as to how far I could go in the Army. He further pointed out that depriving myself of an education, I was also depriving my family from what they could become. He began to make sense. I thought about going back to school many times. If I did, I would have to give up traveling and working as a cameraman. I was afraid that it would take a long time to finish and that I may lose my job in the process. "You can do this", Jim said. "But only if you are willing to work hard and sacrifice". Work hard and sacrifice. That's all I had to do to become more successful. It sounded too easy. But, the fact was, that it wasn't going to be so easy. I had not been in school for a long time. There was so much that I had forgotten. I would have to re-learn many things I learned in school several years ago.

In my heart I knew Jim was right. I knew I would have to give up traveling and shooting motion pictures for a while and go back to school. I knew that my future in the Army depended on my making this sacrifice. Then I decided it was time for me to finish high school. It was going to be hard work, but I knew this high school diploma was going to open many doors which would otherwise remain closed.

It took only eight weeks to complete the courses I needed to qualify for a GED. Passing with flying colors, my Commanding Officer at the 97th Signal Battalion presented me with a GED certificate. He suggested I mail a copy of the GED certificate to my high school in Ville Platte in exchange for a High School diploma. Several weeks went by, then, one day I received a round package in the mail. It was a High School diploma from Sacred Heart High School with my name on it. It was the proudest day of my life. No longer a high school drop out...I was a High School Graduate. The pride consumed me to tears. But they were happy tears. Jim Robinson wept also. Again I experienced the good feeling of success. That following Saturday, Amy and I walked to the center of the Schoenaich village, pushing Sherry in her baby carriage. Every Saturday morning we visited the bakery and butcher for meat and bread. That Saturday, the walk seemed so much more pleasant than before. I had more reason to be proud and I could feel it. Somehow, the air felt richer. The experience of graduating from high school had changed me. I looked up at the clouds, and, for some strange reason, they felt closer, and more inviting. I was a high school graduate, and for that reason, I knew that some day I would see the other side of the clouds.

In May of 1966, I was unexpectedly ordered back to the United States. My orders were for me to report to Fort Lee, Virginia immediately.

I was stationed at Fort Lee for almost a year when I received orders to Vietnam. I was granted a thirty day leave which I used to move Amy and Sherry to Ville Platte, my home town, where they could be looked after by my Mother and others while I was at war in Vietnam. It was a year of pure hell for Amy, but not much more could have been done.

When I stepped off the plane at Tan Sun Nut Air Base in Saigon, the humidity was so heavy it was like breathing water. And the air had a foul stench to it. It felt like I had a lump of phlegm in my throat, like I swallowed the blob. I had three days at the 90th Replacement Company, then, I reported to the 199th Infantry Brigade to begin Redcatcher training. After two weeks of learning how to survive as a Redcatcher, I was assigned the Headquarters Company to head up the photo platoon. My training as a Special Warfare Combatant at Fort Leonard Wood served me well, as I would often be on patrol with the Long Range Reconnaissance Patrol, or **'LRRP'** (pronounced LURP). Their mission was not to engage the enemy, but to spy on him and report intelligence to headquarters. My mission was to photographically record the missions.

December 6, 1967 was a day that changed my life. It was to be a very common eagle flight, eight UH1B helicopter troop transports, enough to move seventy or eighty combat-loaded men. It was to be a short helicopter ride and a walk through the rice paddies. Simply hit the landing zone (lz) and sweep the area clear of any Viet Cong that might be in the area. A firefight was not expected; in fact this mission was deemed so benign, that our catholic Chaplain, Chaplain Angelo Martinez was allowed to go on the flight. Every evening at the command briefing, the Chaplain asked permission to be on the next day's operation, and everyday he was denied. Finally, this mission seemed so safe I think the General would have allowed his mother to board that helicopter. Chaplain Martinez was a soldier's friend. When he could not get the troops to attend Sunday Services, he visited the Enlisted Men's club, not to preach, but to listen. Many of the men suffered from anxiety, some from fear, and many of them were strung out on drugs. Angelo Martinez sat with them, sometime enjoying a beer, and offered an ear and an understanding heart. He always had a story to tell. He could make light of any situation. He often poked fun at himself as a way to be on the same level as the troops. He made them laugh, and helped them forget their troubles, even for just a little while. Everyone knew him, and everyone liked and respected him. He was a soldier's Chaplain.

When the choppers arrived at the landing zone, the door-gunners opened fire at the tree line. We called the Viet Cong 'Charlie'. If Charlie were in there, they were being sprayed with a hail of bullets. When we reached the ground, we scattered in all directions. Each rifle squad was assigned a zone and we headed for that area. The Chaplain and I were told to stay with the company commander and the first sergeant. The choppers finished unloading their cargo of men and lifted off to return to base. Suddenly, all was very quiet. Then the squad leaders began shouting out their commands. "Everybody up, move out!" We were headed for that tree line to begin a sweep of the area. Then the silence was shattered by the roar of AK-47 automatic machinegun fire. Several men fell immediately. Men were being hit from the front, the rear and both sides. It was quickly discovered that we were surrounded. The landing zone was in the middle of a North Vietnam Army base camp. I don't know how many there were, but we were surely out-numbered by many times our numbers

The radio transmitter operator (RTO) began calling for gunship assistance and medevac helicopters. More soldiers were hit as the firing grew heavier. Chaplain Martinez ran to pull a wounded man to safety, then another and another. Only a few minutes had passed before the first medevac helicopters arrived, but it seemed like hours. The gun fire was so loud, and the screaming of wounded men pierced my ears into numbness. We were under attack, receiving fire from all directions. I saw the Chaplain moving yet another wounded man when he himself got hit. I went over to where he was and discovered that he had been hit three or four times, and he continued to run towards the cry of screaming men. I helped Chaplain Martinez load the wounded onto the medevac chopper, when he collapsed. He had lost so much blood he could not stand. The company commander ordered me on to the helicopter also. "Take care of the Chaplain," he shouted. On the way to the 40th Medevac hospital, I administered first aid to the Chaplain. There wasn't much I could do. I had used his first aid wrap to cover his wounds. But there were many wounds and I thought he might bleed to death before we arrived at the 40th medevac. There were other men on the chopper who were very badly shot up. They were probably going to die. I used the first aid wrap from two of the other men to try to save the Chaplain. I was trying to stop the bleeding as best I could. I was covered with blood and none of it was my own. His fate was no longer in my hands. I didn't die that day, and I don't know why. Chaplain Angelo Martinez was treated at the 40th medevac then he was flown to Japan where he recovered. He was awarded the Medal of Honor for his bravery under fire and total disregard for his own safety while saving the lives of wounded men. A few days later when things quieted down, I looked back to what had happened and I knew I would not die in Vietnam. I had been spared because I had things yet to accomplish. I had not yet seen the other side of the clouds.

On May 29, 1968, I boarded a plane bound for San Francisco. My Vietnam tour was complete and I was returning home to Amy and my three year old daughter, Sherry.

The plane finally landed at San Francisco airport after a long eighteen hour flight. The flight attendants had been very good to us. They knew where we had been and that we were anxious to get home. To help pass the time during the long flight, we were given free drinks, all that we wanted.

The flight attendants had purchased several paperback novels, every kind of magazines, current newspapers from all over the country. They sat and talk with us. "Where are you from"? "What's your wife's name"? "Do you have any children"?

We had been given decks of cards. Some of the men were playing Gin, others playing Poker, Spades, or Hearts. And others were just sleeping. I was simply dreaming of getting home. As I looked out the window, I could see a heavy layer of thick clouds below. They seemed the same as they did from the ground. They still held their mystery of what was on the other side. The clouds seem to always be hiding something from me. How was I ever going to find out what was on the other side? The scenes of the Navy jets at Toko-Ri continued to haunt me. I could see them bursting through the clouds below flying gracefully through the empty sky.

After landing, we were bussed to the Oakland Army terminal for processing back into the United States. The buildings across the road were barracks filled with men who were processing to go to Vietnam. Only a year ago, I was in that building. I was being processed to go to war in Vietnam. I just left Amy and Sherry at the New Orleans airport where we said our good byes. As I looked at that building across the road, and saw those men who were on their way to war, I felt all of the anguish I felt a year ago. I thought only of Amy and Sherry and how I missed them. My heart felt heavy with the longing to be with them again. I wept in my pillow many nights thinking about them and wanting to be with them. And now, it would soon be over and I would be home.

The processing took a long time, but, it was necessary. I was fitted with a new uniform. None of the clothes we had in Vietnam were kept. All of our clothing were collected and destroyed. My new uniform was perfectly tailored with new stripes and the ribbons I had been awarded. I didn't even know I had been awarded these medals, but they gave me a chest full of them. I had a brand new pair of shoes, got the first really hot shower in a long time. When finished processing, some of the guys and I were invited into the mess hall where we were served a steak dinner with all of the trimmings including California Napa Valley wine. It was about 7:30 p.m. when dinner was over. We were escorted to a taxi which took us to the San Francisco airport for our flight home. I had to fly to Dallas first, then, take a flight to Lake Charles, Louisiana.

When I stepped off the plane, I saw Amy and Sherry. Amy was wearing a bright yellow and white sun dress, but the colors of her dress were pale comparing to the brilliant smile she was wearing. She ran to me. There are no words to describe what I felt. I was so grateful that she and Sherry were well and safe. I didn't want to ever let go of her again.

Sherry shied away from me. Sherry knew I was 'Daddy', but she didn't know me yet. "Sherry is just a little scared right now", Amy said. "She will come to you soon. She has to get to know you". My mother and my sister Joe were there also. My mother held me so tightly. "My Baby, My Baby!" That's all she could cry out.

When we got home, Amy asked me what I wanted to eat. "Whatever you want!" she said. "A bologna and tomato sandwich with lots of mayonnaise and a tall glass of cold milk!" "That's what I want!" She couldn't believe it. But, that's what she fixed.

I was home for only a few days when I heard the news on the radio of Robert F. Kennedy being shot to death. Robert Kennedy, the brother of the slain President John F. Kennedy was running for the Democratic nomination for President of the United States. He had been fatally shot in California. The news made me tremble. The sounds of war and men dying rang loudly in my head once again. It was sad time for our country once again. Every evening we watched the news on television and listen as the news anchormen announced the number of American soldiers who died in Vietnam. It was a sad time indeed.

We stayed in Ville Platte for about three weeks then headed west for Utah. My next assignment was the Dugway Proving Grounds in Utah. This was the place where the Army accidentally dropped deadly chemicals on a sheep ranch and killed 600 head of sheep. It was the site where CBS filmed its first episode of "60 Minutes" with Mike Wallace and Harry Reasoner. I would be filming some of these chemical tests.

We headed west driving through the long and dreary dry Pan Handle of Texas. Just before we reached the state of Oklahoma, we drove through a sand storm. The cloud of dust and sand was so thick I couldn't see the front of the car. It was slow going and we lost a lot of time. Then, finally, just as quickly as it had begun, it had stopped. Soon we entered into Oklahoma, but for only a few miles, then, we were in southern Colorado. I wanted to get as far as Colorado Springs. There we stayed in a motel for the night. I had the opportunity to call my friend Jim Robinson.

I called directory assistance and asked for 'Jim Robinson'. There was no listing for Jim Robinson. I asked for his brother, Daniel and received a number. When I called, a young girl answered the phone. "Hello, can you help me? I am trying to get in touch with Jim Robinson!" "I don't know a Jim Robinson" the girl said. "Could I speak to your father or mother please?" Her mother took the phone and asked "can I help you?" "Yes," I said.

And I asked about Jim. "My brother-in law's name is James Daryl Robinson!" "Is that who you mean?" "Yes!" "How can I get in touch with him?" "We served in the Army together!" "I'm sorry to have to tell you this, but Daryl was killed in a vehicle accident last year!" My heart felt like it had just been ripped out of me. I couldn't believe my friend, to whom I will be forever grateful for encouraging me to return to school and complete a GED, was dead. I have carried the memory of him, and the fun and frolics we had in Germany, and I will remember him forever.

Dugway Proving Grounds proved to be a very unexciting assignment for me. There was little photographic work to do, except when there was a chemical test going on. Even then, the whole thing was not very interesting and unappealing. On test day, we were expected to be on station as early as 5:00a.m. The test may not be scheduled until 10:00 a.m., but we had to be there anyway, according to the chief engineer in charge. There was a lot of "hurry up and wait", and a lot of government money being wasted. This was the type of mentality and attitude that led to the six hundred sheep being killed earlier that year. Engineers were under pressure to get projects completed, then got somewhat complacent with their responsibilities, and that led to mistakes, which led to disaster. I didn't like the assignment and I was looking forward to a transfer. I didn't have to wait long. A Reserve Sergeant First Class stationed at Fort Douglas, in Salt Lake City was retiring and the command needed a replacement for him. Since I was the senior enlisted person in photo at Dugway, it was natural that I got the job.

I became the Classified Custodian for all classified photographs and motion picture film for the Desert Test Center. I did that job until my enlistment was complete in January of 1969 when I was discharged from the Army. After a brief stay at Univac Corporation in Salt Lake City where I worked as an illustrative photographer, we moved to St. Joseph, Michigan, where I worked for Whirlpool Corporation as a Service Training Coordinator.

My work at Whirlpool offered me many challenges, more so than at Dugway Proving Grounds. At Whirlpool, I was assisting eight Service Training Administrators who had the responsibility of producing training programs on the appliances built by Whirlpool Corporation. These training programs required a large amount of critical photography. The first few months I worked with inadequate equipment. The camera was not designed to do the critical work that was required. It didn't take me long to convince the director of the training center that a more specific camera was needed to do this job. Soon I was authorized to purchase the needed equipment. With the new camera, I was able to tell the administrators, "If you can see it, I can take a picture of it!"

The improved camera system directly improved the quality of training programs and the director received many favorable reports from the field. The District Managers using the training materials were extremely excited about the new products. Needless to say, I made my mark at Whirlpool. And again, success felt very good.

The winters in Michigan were long and harsh. The summers were fun, because we lived in a small community called Stevensville which was only about a mile from the Lake Michigan. We lived near Lake Michigan where we visited the beach which we enjoyed all summer long, or I should say, "All summer short", because the summers were...very short. The day after Labor Day, the wind turned briskly to the north, and the temperature dropped dramatically. By the end of October, the snow was flying. In December, we had twenty four to thirty inches of snow on the ground which was there until late May.

But, we made the most of it. Warren Dunes State Park was near by also. The sand dunes rose for forty or fifty feet above the beach. In deep winter the water of Lake Michigan froze at the shores. The sport was to ride toboggans from the top of the dunes down on to the beach, and slide on to the frozen lake. Sherry and I took our toboggan to the top of the dunes as high as we could go, then push ourselves off and slide at tremendous speed down to the frozen lake where we finally came to a stop. Oh my, what fun it was to see Sherry laugh so much and have so much fun. How I treasure those times with her. It was like an endless fantasy land. She laughed so loudly. When we reached the lake bed and stop, she cried out, "again Daddy, let's do it again!" What a time we had.

Another hallmark for Amy and I was giving birth to Andre Michelle. She was born on April 5th, 1971. To our surprise, she had invaded our world about six weeks early. That morning, Amy got up before I did, and began floundering around the apartment causing all kinds of racket. I emerged from the bedroom and discovered her at the kitchen table sewing on a housecoat. I asked what she was doing. She told me her water broke and Andre was about to be born. She said needed a house coat to wear at the hospital. We quickly packed her things, placed Sherry with a friend for the day, and I drove her to the hospital. Andre was born about 10:00 a.m. that day. The very next day, the Pediatrician discovered a problem. Andre could not swallow. A barium swallow revealed that her esophagus had not formed properly and was attached to her lung rather than her stomach and she required immediate surgery to correct the problem. She weighed only four and half pounds at birth, and the specialists didn't give her much of a chance to survive. I took her by ambulance to Motts Children Hospital in Ann Arbor Michigan where specialist dealt with her kind of problem everyday. I was greeted by a Dr. Gaston who explained all of the details of the surgery, and that Andre was in good hands. Later I found out by one of the surgeon assistants that Dr. Gaston was the foremost authority on this particular surgery. Whether this guy was telling me this to comfort me at the time became irrelevant when we brought Andre home seven weeks later, a healthy happy baby.

The years passed quickly, and I continued to reach new heights of accomplishments at Whirlpool. But something was missing. I was being challenged, but the challenges were too easily accomplished. The work was mundane. Taking pictures of switches and controls on washing machines and refrigerators was not the type of photography I wanted to do. I wanted to create motion pictures. I wanted to film action. My frustration must have been quite evident, because my supervisor could see it. Amy could see it also. They could tell that I was unhappy in what I was doing because the excitement of the challenge was gone. My work was too routine. I needed to be in the military again, and Amy knew it. So, one day she just said it…"Go, get back in the Army, you know that is what you want!"

I called the Army recruiter the next day.

There was a problem. I could re-enlist in the Army, but I would have to forfeit all of my previous rank, and go through basic training again as a new recruit. The United States had ended the war with North Vietnam and the Army was not looking for new recruits. The Army simply was not interested in someone in my category having previous service, high rank and three dependents in spite of my experience. I wasn't going to give up that easily. I wanted to be in the military to be a motion picture cameraman again. I decided to take my problem all the way to the top.

I wrote the President of the United States and two Congressmen, asking them why a soldier of my skill and abilities was being denied entry into the army. The recruiting office received a Presidential and two Congressional inquiries as to "why this person was writing the President and what was the problem". I didn't get into the Army, but the Navy made me an offer that was too hard to refuse.

The Navy was building two super aircraft carriers, the *USS Nimitz,* and the *USS Eisenhower.* The two super carriers would need several hundred men, specifically middle grade petty officers. The Navy recruiter called and offered me a job in the Navy.

Chapter Six

The United States Navy

*A*fter reporting to Norfolk Naval Air Station and settling in the command, I was informed the chief petty officer in charge of operations that the Navy was looking for motion picture cameramen with combat experience to fly in jets and make movies of jets…and asked if I would be interested in doing that. It took a while for me to absorb what was being said, and I know I asked the chief to repeat what he had said, several times…and just could not believe what I was hearing. A dream, I dreamed years ago when I was but a nine year old child was about to become true. How often did I stare at the clouds wondering what was on the other side? My heart raced with excitement. The scenes of those brave Navy pilots flying the jets through the sky played in my mind over and over again. I am going to be in one of those planes as a Navy aerial cameraman. "Would I be interested in that?" The question rang in my head. "Hell yes I would be interested in doing that!" "When can I start?" "Immediately," was the answer. I knew that I had the ability to be a good aerial cameraman, a great cameraman…"I would become the best aerial cameraman in the Navy!"

Before I could fly in the back seat of jets I had to receive special training in physiology. The lessons explained the effect of high altitude supersonic flight has on the human body. It involved learning breathing techniques while wearing a mask and taking in 100% oxygen. High altitudes in high performance jets aircraft can cause bubbles to form in the blood stream called the bends. This can be very painful and sometime debilitating. It can cause pilots to black out and lose control of the aircraft.

The training also included water survival. Every part of this training was designed to fail those who could not contend with the physical constraints as well as the mental and intellectual conditions of the training. The pressure chamber was challenging, but not near as demanding as the swimming pool where we had to tread water and stay afloat for twenty minutes wearing full flight suits and boots. It was the thirty foot tower that washed out most candidates. For me, it was just another jump in the irrigation canal.

Chapter Seven

My First Flight

*M*y first flight was in a Navy TA4 trainer. The A4 is a Navy fighter designed to protect the aircraft carrier from enemy air attack. It is very small and sleek and extremely fast. The TA4, having two seats, is the model used to train pilots. My first mission was to take a series of still photos and motion pictures of an F-14 section. A section consisted of two aircraft, the mission commander and his wingman. I was to portray them in several different combat maneuver configurations. It was a challenge because I didn't know what combat configurations were. But I soon learned.

Fortunately for me the pilot of the TA4 was a really good guy. He asked if we could meet at least an hour before the flight to brief on the mission and get to know one another. This helped tremendously because I was so nervous I could have crapped in my pants. God, I was so scared it was all I could do to control my shaking body. My mind was numb. I couldn't even ask a stupid question even if I had to. The pilot was Lt. Miller. He was great. He was from a little town called Franklin, just outside Nashville, Tennessee. He graduated from Tennessee State and had a Masters in Avionics. He told me that I should relax, that he would be in control of the events at all times and that all I had to do was to concentrate on the photography and that all would be fine. Then, in an effort to be funny, or to maybe place me more at ease, he asked, "Is this your first flight in a Navy Jet?" Yes! I answered. "OK, don't worry about it!" "We will have some fun!" Then he said, "We will have about forty five minutes with nothing to do while the F-14s complete their assigned missions." "If you like, I can give you the stick and you can fly around for a while on your own." I couldn't believe what I was hearing. I was going to hold the stick of a Navy jet in my hands and fly through the empty sky, free, like a bird. I could not hold back the question. I simply had to ask Lt. Miller if I could fly to a height that allowed me to see the other side of the clouds. He simply said, "That is one of my favorite things to do."

The inside of the cockpit is a lot smaller then it seems from the outside. I felt like it just fit me perfectly, like it had been made just for me. How did some of those big guys get in this tightfisted space I wondered? I had not climbed into the cockpit, I was wearing an airplane. It felt like a snug jacket. One of the plane captains assisted me in the seat. He pulled out the ejection system safety pins and warned me that my seat was now armed and I could eject in the event of trouble. He then connected my oxygen mask hose to the aircraft system and asked me to breathe normally. The mask worked as designed and I was ready to go. My mind was filled with amazement and inquisitiveness as I scanned the interior of the cockpit. It was an enclosure, like an envelope of buttons, switched and gauges and instruments. How could anyone remain aware of this mass of contrivance and still fly the plane?

The excitement increased as we taxied the plane towards the runway. I was filled with anticipation and trembling, shaking. My mouth was dry I could hardly swallow. Finally, we reached the end of the runway and Lt. Miller turned the aircraft pointing straight down the long stretch of concrete. It seemed endless as the contours of this long concrete ribbon converged to a point in the far distance. The plane stopped. Lt. Miller alerted the control tower that flight zero nine-alpha was ready for takeoff. This was the moment I had been longing for. A boyhood dream was only seconds away from becoming a reality. On this day I would finally see the other side of the clouds.

Lt. Miller pushed the throttle forward and the engine roared as the plane began rolling down the runway. Fast, then, faster and louder, and faster. The ecstasy was intensifying with every passing second. I was in a Navy jet aircraft rolling down the runway heading for the open sky. The pressure from the acceleration was pushing against my chest as the plane rolled faster and faster down the long runway. My thoughts were empty. I felt nothing but jubilance and total rapture. Then, he pulled back on the stick and I felt the plane rise, and the nose pointed straight into the sky and I could feel the sensation of acceleration as we climbed higher and higher into the deep blue sky. I felt as light as a feather as we climbed higher and higher into the bright blue emptiness. I could feel my heart pounding in my chest. I had never before experienced anything so delightful in my life. It felt like my heart was going to burst right out of my body. The vibration of the engine and the power of thrust pushing on me felt so exciting. I didn't want it to end.

When we reached an altitude of 30,000 feet, Lt Miller leveled off the flight, and I heard him tell the tower that he was turning to a heading of 090 toward the training area and that he was climbing to an altitude of 40,000 feet. I could see heavy high clouds on the horizon and wondered if those were the clouds I would visit that day. Were those the clouds that would finally reveal their secrets to me? My heart shook as I thought about it. Finally I would be amongst the clouds and see the other side. Lt. Miller instructed me to take control of the plane and begin to fly. Nervously, and reluctantly, I grabbed hold of the stick. I didn't do anything, I just held it. "Fly the plane" he said. "Turn left and head for that cloud formation out there". "Just push the left rudder pedal slightly until you have made your turn, then, let it back slowly".

The highest of the large cumulus clouds must have been at least fifty thousand feet high. That was the one I wanted to reach. Lt. Miller instructed me to push the throttle forward and ease back on the stick to create a smooth gentle climb. Soon we were at the level of my cloud and he said, "Simply fly smoothly around it," "Touch it with your wing." "Follow its contour." "Be gentle with it." The feeling of being there was indescribable. It was like tasting something very delectable for the first time. There were no words to explain the feeling of fulfillment and accomplishment. After so many years of wondering what lay beyond, I had seen the other side of the clouds. And I discovered that the cloud, that majestic illusive beautiful untouchable cloud was nothing but condensed air.

I flew many more missions after this flight with Lt. Miller, many with some different degrees of success. I was good at what I was doing, because I loved doing it so much. But I knew something was missing. I wasn't as good as I knew I could be. I still did not have all of the knowledge and training and experience to be a good Aerial Cameraman, a Great Aerial Cameraman...indeed, the best Aerial Cameraman.

When I received that High School Diploma from Sacred Heart High School, I experienced success. I also received the confidence of achievement. I wanted to move mountains, and change things from what they were, because of the way they were. I had experienced many successes since, and I had become addicted to the wonderful feeling of success. In our command, we had a man by the name of Tim Connors. Tim had the reputation of being the best aerial cameraman in the Navy. When requests for aerial motion pictures were ordered for our command to produce, the requesters were asking for Petty Officer Tim Connors. I wanted to change that. I wanted to be requested as the preferred aerial cameraman to fly that job. I needed to become better. I needed to know what was required to be the best. So, I asked Tim one day if he would help me become a better aerial cameraman. Tim agreed, and for the next three months, I worked with him, learning new equipment, new techniques, and we flew every chance we could. One of the best advices Tim gave me was this. "You have an assignment to photograph an event that probably will not occur again, and, it will cost thousands of dollars to do one time." "Your mission is to successfully record this event, the first time." "When you enter that aircraft with that kind of mission, you must inform the entire aircraft crew of your mission, and when the aircraft arrives on station for that event, YOU are in charge of the aircraft and the crew will adhere to your commands." "You must make that clear with every member of the crew." "When the aircraft is in position to perform the elements of your mission, it is your responsibility to direct the aircraft crew, with whom you are flying, and any other aircraft and aircraft crew, associated with the outcome of your mission." "Any failure of any aircraft crew personnel involved with this mission is answerable to the Chief of Naval Operations, according to the provisions stipulated in Air Operations Directive 1411." "In other words, when your aircraft arrives at the point which begins your photographic mission, you are God."

I had no trouble understanding what Petty Officer Connors was telling me. I am responsible for my mission.

With that stern advice, I briefed the pilots before each mission. I made sure that they clearly understood what I had to do to complete my job. We talked about the strategy and course and discussed alternative actions in the event of problems. The pre-mission briefings yielded good teamwork and many successful jobs.

Tim trained me well. Then one day, out of the blue (as it were) came the job that people who did what I did, only dream of. The Department of the Navy had a request to produce a film which was to be used in a Navy aircraft simulator. This simulator was to travel by way of the Navy Recruit Command to colleges and universities across the

United States in an effort to recruit young men and women into the Naval Aviation program. This film was to be perfect. It required launching off an aircraft carrier, flying in formation with F-14s, F-18s, in-flight refueling, aerial simulated combat, combat maneuvers and carrier landings. And the job was for one aerial cameraman only. I got the job.

I flew aboard the carrier USS America where I worked for the following two weeks. My aircraft was an A6D which was the perfect platform for this job because the pilot and radar-navigator sat side by side, both having a frontal view of the flight. I had to design a special camera mount to fit into the cockpit so that I could pan and tilt the camera smoothly. I flew two, two hour missions every day for two weeks. At the end of each day, my body had taken every kind of beating one can imagine. The physiological stress of high altitude, high speed flight is tremendously brutal on the human body. That is why only young men and women can perform these tasks.

At the end of my two week cruise with the USS America I returned to Norfolk, and in about two weeks, the film I had shot returned from the lab in D.C. Every Monday morning, our Commanding Officer held film screening with the entire command. When a cameraman's film was about to be screened, that cameraman stands and faces the CO, and explains the mission he or she filmed. When I stood to introduce my film, I called it "the mission from hell!" (Because of the amount of grueling flying that was required each day.) "The Navy Recruit Command Project aboard the USS America, filmed by PH2 Weldon J. Dupuis!" The film ran continuously for five hours. When the projector lamp turned dark, and the house lights came on, there wasn't a word uttered. Finally, the CO spoke. "Is Tim Connors in the room?" "Yes sir!" "Tim answered!" "Tim, you are an excellent cameraman, and you have been at the top of your profession for a long time!" "But, I think you will agree that, this time, you have been out gunned!" "We have a new TOP GUN!"

Chapter Eight

USC
School of Cinema
Arts

*O*ne of the Navies's training programs allowed for the top one percent of cinematographers of the command personnel to attend the University of Southern California to study cinema for one year. After delivering aerial footage that unseated a reigning champion like Tim Connors, I had no reason to believe that I would not be selected to attend USC that year. The selection of motion picture cameramen to attend USC was the responsibility of a board set up by the office of the Chief of Naval Operations. That board was headed by none other than Lieutenant Commander Marquez. The same person, who in Public Affairs ordered the film for the Naval Air Simulator, saw my request for USC and set my records aside, then, informed the other board members that they had to select twelve candidates to attend USC, and that he had made the first selection and they had eleven to go. I had automatically been selected to attend USC without my records even being reviewed. This was highly unusual because only the most successful cinematographers were to be selected for this training. The records of all candidates should be screened for qualification. Lt. Commander Marquez knew of my qualifications and he assured the board that I was the top choice. Once again, I had seen the other side of the clouds. From that day on, everything I did led to success.

At USC, I, and the rest of the military students were sadly and brutally informed the military was not welcomed at this university, and that we were not to expect much cooperation from the faculty. It seems that it was a consensus of opinion among the faculty that the military people, based upon past performances of past participants, were not qualified for this school, showed below average rate of intelligence, and were there just to have some fun and learn nothing. This is the stigma with which the military class of 1976 was stuck. Some of the instructors had posted notes on the bulletin board that they did not want to teach military classes. We had only one instructor who was willing to give us a chance, and if it had not been for him, the program at USC just might have shut down. I was ashamed to learn that my fellow sailors, who had preceded me to that prestigious university, had behaved in such a manner that the faculty refused to teach future candidates. Later, with the one instructor came another, then another. But, they didn't seem too enthusiastic to teach us.

The twelve of us candidates, which included two officers, knew that we had to do something and change the opinions and attitudes of these USC instructors. We organized. And from that organization emerged, The Big Three. The Big Three were the strongest leaders who guided the military class to success and change the opinions and attitudes of the people of USC who thought that the military students were there only for a free ride and a free year off from the military. We were determined to prove that the military students could out perform civilian students any day. The Big Three were, Bill Scallan, Steve Wilder and Joe Dupuis. Together we pulled our troops into work study groups, we formed teams and encouraged competition between teams, and monitored each other's progress to make sure that no one fell between the cracks.

By the end of the second semester, all three teams had completed films to composite print, which meant that the picture and the sound track were united on to one piece of film. No other military class had ever done that in the history of the Navy-USC program. Yes, our class turned some heads and changed some opinions about the military at USC. The instructors who had posted negative notes about the military on the bulletin board removed their notes and wanted to teach the military classes. Our films from the second semester were viewed as some of the best to be done at USC. All of the Navy films were being showcased as triumphant examples of excellent work. The Big Three had done their work.

USC had been a challenge for me because I hadn't been a full time college student before. I had taken a course now and then, but never full time. It was a good experience which added to the overall intellectual development of my character and leadership abilities. When I returned to Norfolk Naval Air Station, and the Atlantic Fleet Audio Visual Command, I was in charge of a camera crew as crew chief. It was then that the culmination of all that I learned in my life served to help me reach the pinnacle of my career.

During the summer of 1977, the Navy planned a cruise involving three destroyers. The ships were to sail down the St. Lawrence River by way of Quebec, Canada, into the great Lakes. The cruise was to be a recruiting exercise to expose the Navy to the people of the Great Lakes Region. The ships made several port calls, and the sailors met a lot of people.

I was chosen to film that cruise and produce a documentary film. My crew and I were aboard the ships for three weeks. We departed the ships in Detroit and flew back to Norfolk. A few months later, my film about the Great

Lakes Cruise was submitted for competition at the United States Armed Forces Film Awards held at the University of Oklahoma. The films were being judged by professional film director, producers, and news directors from all over the country. The Great Lakes Cruise documentary was selected as a top film and in 1977 I was selected as the United States Armed Forces Motion Picture Cameraman of the Year. Later that year, I was selected for promotion to Chief Petty Officer.

Before being promoted to Chief, my crew and I were assigned a six month tour to Sigonella Air Base in Sicily, Italy. From this base we would serve the naval commands in Europe and the Mediterranean areas to include some parts of the Middle East. We left for our assignment in January of 1978.

The Naval Motion Picture School at Pensacola, Florida was not doing a very good job at training the young sailors for fleet operations. The command at Norfolk saw this as a real problem. The command could not send those sailors back to school for more training and was given permission to start its own school. But who was to create this school and operate it? "The best man for this job is in Sigonella," someone told the Commanding Officer. "Who do you mean?" asked the CO. "Petty Officer Dupuis sir!" "He is the best we have!" "Bring him back!" the CO ordered. Within a few days I was on my way back to Norfolk to build The Atlantic Fleet Motion Picture School. The films that my fellow students and I made at USC became instructional aids for my new students. My assignment was to construct a lesson plan and prepare those sailors for operational duty in the Atlantic Fleet. The following several weeks were dedicated to developing lesson plans for training. I started the school which was needed by the command and soon, the fleet was being served by well trained knowledgeable photographers.

The next seven years I was assigned to various positions as 'The Chief'

My final duty station was Naval Air Station, Bermuda. I was in charge of a small photo facility. This assignment was perfect for my next accomplishment. The Navy started me on a college program by sending me to USC for a year. In Bermuda I had the opportunity to complete a college education. I began first with only one course, then two courses, and finally after two years, I graduated from the University Of Maryland with a Bachelor of Science degree in Radio and Television. I completed yet another major task. I felt the sting of failure as a high school drop out and learned that failure is not the end, but the beginning of a new opportunity. I also learned the joy of success as a college graduate. I retired from the Navy after a four year assignment in Bermuda.

I discovered that the other side of the clouds is not a place, but an event. An achievement reached by having a vision and setting goals, working hard and being willing to sacrifice. The other side of the clouds was a dream after seeing the movie of jet fighters flying gracefully through the sky. The clouds were an achievement needed prove to myself that I could succeed. My father had to know that I wasn't a failure. It gave me great pleasure to explain to him what I had accomplished in my life; an accomplished and elite soldier, an honored and esteemed craftsman, and had elevated myself to the top of my profession. His greatest pride came when he learned that I had earned a college degree. He didn't understand what it meant for me being a motion picture cameraman and being the best. Nor did he understand why I was flying in jets making movies of jets. He did appreciate the value and honor of a college education. My father was proud of me. And that might very well be my greatest accomplishment.

The other side of the clouds was a goal needed to be realized, one that required hard work, planning and achievement. The other side of the clouds was a goal set to be attained at all cost and personal investment. It took a long time and the help of many people, like Jim Robinson who believed that I could be anything I wanted to be. Like Amy, who was willing to give her understanding and have faith in me. She sacrificed her personal goals that I could have the opportunity to succeed in my career.

The other side of the clouds was a dream that formed itself in my mind while lying in the clover field a long time ago. The other side of the clouds drove me to be what I needed to be.

The old house in the field where I laid in the clover watching the clouds is gone. The irrigation ponds, the canals, they are all gone. Only the clouds remain. They remind me from where I came and who I was. They tell me what I have done and what I have become. They hold the memories of all the people who entered my life and had a hand at steering me through my successes and accomplishments. They are a constant reminder, that all things are possible. Anyone can be whatever it is one wants to be. If one is willing to do only two things…work hard and sacrifice. I have seen the other side of the clouds and they hold secrets from me no more. The clouds gave me a dream, but didn't tell me how to accomplish that dream. I had to learn that for myself. Many people had a direct impact on my life, and provided me with a means to fulfill my dream. Early failures in my life provided me with additional opportunities to succeed. To dream a dream is part of growing up. It is a part of life. But, a dream without goals is only a wish. Wishes do not come true. Work hard and sacrifice is the only way to success. For me, the dream was to see the other side of the clouds. What will be your dream? How will you know for what to strive? My love was for movies. Movies were magical wonders that titillated my heart each time I watched. Failing high school suspended my dream and held it in check until I could experience success. Successes like completing Army Basic Training and Special Warfare Training School lead the way to my completing high school and completing a college degree then brought back my dream. A dream is only a dream without goals.

If you are in school, stay in school. Work harder and seek help from those who can help you. Everyone has a Jim Robinson in their life. Find him! Believe him! Trust him! If you are no longer in school, go back. Your school system has many avenues to help you complete your high school education. If you stop now, then you will continually be looking back with regret, and you will have reached the pinnacle of your success. Your dreams without a vision and goals are only wishes and wishes do not come true. You are the only person in the world who can make the critical decision that will offer you a chance to be a success in life. Don't cheat yourself. Failure is not the end. Believe in yourself and make today the first day of your new beginning. The other side of the clouds is not a place. The other side of the clouds is success and the fulfillment of dreams.